THE TRADER'S EDGE

THE TRADER'S EDGE

A Strategy Playbook for Reading Price,
Managing Risk, and Trading with Discipline

Markeese Phelps

This book is for educational purposes only and does not constitute financial, investment, or trading advice. Day trading carries substantial risk of loss and is not suitable for everyone. Past performance and backtested results do not guarantee future outcomes. Always do your own research and consider consulting a licensed financial professional before trading with real capital.

First Edition

Contents

1. The Trader's Mindset

Strategy fails without discipline behind it. Before any chart work, get the operating principles right — they determine whether you follow your edge or sabotage it.

What separates consistent traders from the rest

- Consistent traders treat trading as a business with rules, not a series of bets on hunches.
- They accept that any single trade's outcome is close to random; edge only shows up over a large sample of trades.
- They separate the quality of a decision from the quality of its outcome — a good trade can lose money, a bad trade can win.
- They have a written plan and trade it the same way whether they're up or down for the day.
- They know their max daily/weekly loss before the session starts, not after they've blown through it.

The four failure patterns to eliminate first

Revenge trading

Taking an oversized, low-quality trade immediately after a loss to "get it back." Fix: a hard rule — after two consecutive losses, stop trading for the day or step away for 30 minutes.

Overtrading

Taking setups that don't meet your criteria because you're bored or the market feels active. Fix: a daily trade cap (e.g., 3–5 quality setups) and a checklist every entry must pass.

Moving stops

Widening a stop-loss because you "believe" the trade will turn. This converts a defined-risk trade into an undefined-risk one. Fix: set the stop at entry and treat moving it further away as a rule violation, not a judgment call.

Cutting winners early / letting losers run

Fear of giving back profit closes winners too soon; hope keeps losers open too long. Fix: predefine exits (target, trailing stop, or time stop) before entering, and only reference them, not your emotions, when the trade is live.

Worked example

You're up two solid, plan-following trades this morning. On the third setup, price stops you out by a tick before reversing in your favor. You immediately re-enter double size without a new signal, "to make it back." That's revenge trading — the fix from this chapter (stop after two losses, or step away 30 minutes) applies the moment you notice the impulse, not after the next loss confirms it was a mistake.

Key takeaways

- Edge plays out over a sample of trades, not any single trade — judge your process, not one outcome.
- Know your daily loss limit and trade cap before the market opens.
- Predefine every exit before you enter; the plan should not change once you're in the trade.

2. Market Structure & How Price Really Moves

Every strategy in this book rests on understanding who is on the other side of your trade and why price moves the way it does.

Who moves the market

- Market makers provide liquidity and profit from the bid-ask spread; they don't have directional conviction, they manage inventory.
- Institutional traders (funds, algos) move size over time using execution algorithms (VWAP, TWAP, iceberg orders) to avoid moving price against themselves.
- Retail traders are usually the liquidity institutions trade against — this is why obvious, crowded setups often fail.
- Understanding this hierarchy explains why price often reverses right after it looks "obvious" to retail: that's where liquidity pools for larger players to fill against.

Order flow basics

The order book

Shows resting limit orders (bids below price, asks above). Large resting orders can act as short-term support/resistance, but can also be pulled instantly — don't treat them as guaranteed walls.

Tape (time and sales)

Shows executed trades in real time. Watch for absorption (large sell orders hitting a level without price dropping — buyers are absorbing supply) and exhaustion (price extends on decreasing trade size — the move is running out of participants).

Liquidity pools

Clusters of stop-losses and pending orders tend to sit just beyond obvious highs/lows and round numbers. Price is frequently drawn to these levels to fill large orders before reversing — this is the mechanical reason for stop hunts, not manipulation folklore.

Worked example

Stock XYZ has an obvious daily low at $48.00 that every retail trader on social media is watching as "support." Price dips to $47.92, triggers the resting stop-loss cluster just below that round number, then reverses hard back above $48.50 within minutes. That's not manipulation — it's liquidity: institutional buyers used the stop-run to get filled at a better average price than they could have gotten by buying into $48.00 directly.

Key takeaways

- Price moves to where liquidity is, not just where news or sentiment points.
- Obvious retail setups are often the liquidity institutions trade against — expect fakeouts at crowded levels.
- Use tape and order book context to confirm a level is holding, not just that it exists on a chart.

3. Support, Resistance & Supply/Demand Zones

Levels are the backbone of every entry and exit decision. Draw them wrong and every downstream strategy inherits the error.

Drawing levels correctly

- Use zones, not single lines — mark the range where price reversed (wick-to-wick or body-to-body), not one exact price.
- Prioritize levels with multiple touches and high volume over single-touch levels.
- Weight recent structure more heavily than structure from months ago; markets evolve.
- Round numbers and prior day/week/month highs and lows tend to matter because many participants watch the same levels — this is self-fulfilling, not mystical.

Supply and demand zones vs. classic support/resistance

A supply/demand zone is the last consolidation area before a strong, fast move away from it — evidence that large orders were being filled there. Mark the zone from the base of the move, not just the exact turning candle. These zones are considered "fresh" (higher probability) the first time price returns to them, and weaken with each retest as the resting orders get used up.

Confirming a level before trading it

- Look for a reaction: rejection wicks, decreasing volume into the level, or a shift in candle character (large bodies to small bodies).
- Wait for the first pullback after a breakout rather than chasing the breakout candle itself — this is usually a better risk/reward entry.
- Don't trade a level in isolation — check the higher timeframe trend first (see Chapter 6).

Worked example

A stock rallies sharply off $22.10–$22.30, runs to $25, then pulls back. The first time it returns to the $22.10–$22.30 zone, it shows a rejection wick and volume dries up on the approach — a fresh, high-probability long. Three weeks later the same zone gets tested a fourth time; it barely pauses before breaking through, because the resting orders that defended it early on have already been used up.

Key takeaways

- Mark zones, not exact prices, and weight recent, high-volume, multi-touch levels highest.
- Fresh supply/demand zones (untested since the move away) carry higher probability than repeatedly retested ones.
- Confirm reaction at a level before entering — don't assume it will hold just because it's drawn.

4. Candlestick Patterns That Matter

Most candlestick pattern lists are bloated with low-value noise. This is the short list worth memorizing, plus how to filter out false signals.

High-value patterns

Engulfing candle

A candle whose body fully engulfs the prior candle's body, especially after a stretched move or at a key level. Signals a shift in control between buyers and sellers.

Pin bar / rejection candle

A long wick with a small body at the opposite end, showing price was pushed one direction and aggressively rejected. Most reliable at a marked support/resistance or supply/demand zone — meaningless in the middle of a range.

Inside bar

A candle fully contained within the prior candle's range, showing contraction/indecision. Useful as a low-risk continuation entry when it forms with the trend, with a stop just beyond the inside bar's range.

Three-bar reversal

A strong trend candle, a small-range pause candle, then a strong candle in the opposite direction closing beyond the first candle's midpoint. Confirms a real shift rather than a single-candle head-fake.

Why most other patterns underperform

- Patterns like doji, hammer, or shooting star are far too common to have edge on their own — they need location (at a real level) and context (trend, volume) to mean anything.
- A pattern against the higher-timeframe trend is a much weaker signal than the same pattern with the trend.
- Never trade a pattern in isolation — it's a trigger, not a strategy.

Worked example

Price is falling into a marked demand zone at $14.50–$14.70. The candle that touches $14.52 has a long lower wick and closes near its high — a pin bar. On its own, that candle means little; the same shape appears dozens of times a day in the middle of nowhere. Here, at a real level, with the higher-timeframe trend still up, it's a valid low-risk long trigger with a stop just under $14.50.

Key takeaways

- Fewer, higher-quality patterns beat memorizing dozens of shapes.
- Location (at a real level) and context (trend, volume) turn a pattern into a signal.
- Use patterns as entry triggers within a broader setup, never as a standalone strategy.

5. Volume & Volume Profile

Price tells you what happened; volume tells you how much conviction was behind it. Trading price without volume is trading half the information.

Reading volume in real time

- A breakout on rising volume is far more likely to follow through than one on flat or declining volume.
- A move that stalls on declining volume after an extended trend often signals exhaustion, not necessarily reversal — wait for price confirmation.
- Watch for volume climax: an unusually large volume spike after an extended move can mark a short-term top or bottom as the last buyers/sellers get absorbed.
- Low volume during a pullback within a trend is healthy (profit-taking, not new selling pressure); high volume on a pullback is a warning sign.

Volume profile essentials

Point of Control (POC)

The price level with the highest traded volume in the session/range. Acts as a magnet — price often returns to it, and it can act as support or resistance.

Value Area

The price range containing roughly 70% of the session's volume. Price outside the value area is considered "extended" and more likely to mean-revert back into it, especially in range-bound conditions.

High Volume Nodes (HVN) vs. Low Volume Nodes (LVN)

HVNs are areas of acceptance (price spent a long time there — expect slower movement, more support/resistance). LVNs are areas of rejection (price moved through quickly — expect fast moves when price re-enters this zone).

Worked example

Two identical-looking breakouts above a $30.00 range high: one happens on volume 3x the 20-day average, the other on volume below average. The first tends to follow through because real participation is behind it; the second is a classic trap that often snaps back into the range within minutes. Same chart pattern, opposite outcome — volume is the differentiator.

Key takeaways

- Confirm every breakout with volume — rising volume supports follow-through, flat volume warns of a false move.

- Use POC and value area to judge whether price is "fair" or extended relative to where the session actually traded.
- Low volume nodes tend to produce fast moves; high volume nodes tend to produce chop.

6. Multi-Timeframe Analysis

The timeframe you trade should never be the only timeframe you look at. Context from higher timeframes prevents you from fighting the larger trend.

The three-timeframe framework

- Higher timeframe (e.g., daily/4H): defines the dominant trend and the major levels you should respect.
- Trading timeframe (e.g., 15min/5min): where you build your setup and identify structure within the higher-timeframe context.
- Entry timeframe (e.g., 1min): where you fine-tune entry timing and tighten your stop.
- A trade with the higher timeframe trend at your back has meaningfully better odds than the identical setup against it.

Practical workflow

- Start every session on the daily chart: mark trend direction, major support/resistance, and any key levels from the prior day/week.
- Drop to your trading timeframe to identify the current structure (trend, range, or transition) and mark intraday levels.
- Only drop to the entry timeframe once price reaches a level of interest on the trading timeframe — don't watch the 1-minute chart all day without context.
- If the higher timeframe and trading timeframe disagree, the higher timeframe wins — treat trading-timeframe signals as counter-trend and size down or skip.

Worked example

The daily chart shows a clean uptrend. On the 15-minute chart, price pulls back to a rising trendline and prints a bullish engulfing candle — a valid long setup. Dropping to the 1-minute chart only to time the entry (not to second-guess direction), you enter on the break of the engulfing candle's high with a tight stop just below its low.

Key takeaways

- Always know the higher-timeframe trend before taking a lower-timeframe signal.
- Use the entry timeframe for timing only, not for deciding direction.
- When timeframes conflict, defer to the higher one or stand aside.

7. Trend vs. Chop: Knowing Which Game You're Playing

Trend-following and mean-reversion strategies are opposites. Applying the wrong one to current conditions is one of the fastest ways to lose money.

Identifying a trending market

- Higher highs and higher lows (uptrend) or lower highs and lower lows (downtrend) on your trading timeframe.
- Pullbacks are shallow and get bought/sold quickly; they don't retrace the whole prior move.
- Moving averages are sloped and price respects them on pullbacks (e.g., the 20 or 50 EMA acting as dynamic support in an uptrend).
- ADX (Average Directional Index) above roughly 25 is a common, if rough, numerical filter for trend strength.

Identifying a choppy/ranging market

- Price oscillates between a clear ceiling and floor without making new structural highs/lows.
- Moving averages are flat and get crossed repeatedly — they're not acting as support/resistance.
- Breakout attempts repeatedly fail and snap back into the range ("fakeouts").
- Volume is often lower and less directional than in a trending phase.

Matching strategy to regime

- In a trend: favor breakout/momentum strategies and trend-pullback entries; avoid fading strength.
- In a range: favor mean-reversion strategies at the range boundaries; avoid chasing breakouts until they're confirmed with volume and a retest.
- In transition (trend losing structure, or range boundary breaking): reduce size and wait for the new regime to confirm rather than guessing.

Worked example

ADX on the daily reads 34 and rising with clear higher highs and higher lows — this is trend conditions, so breakout and pullback-long setups get priority. Two weeks later ADX drifts to 14 while price chops between $56 and $59 for ten sessions straight — now mean-reversion setups at $56 and $59 are favored, and breakout attempts above $59 should be treated with suspicion until proven with volume.

Key takeaways

- Identify the regime (trend vs. range) before choosing a strategy, not after.
- Trend strategies and mean-reversion strategies both work — using the wrong one for current conditions is the actual problem.
- Reduce size or stand aside during regime transitions until the new structure confirms.

8. Momentum & Breakout Trading Strategy

A complete, rules-based breakout strategy — the setup, entry, stop, and target, not just the concept.

The setup

- Identify a well-defined consolidation or range (at least 3–5 touches on each boundary) after an initial impulsive move — this is your base.
- Confirm the higher timeframe trend supports the breakout direction (Chapter 6).
- Watch for volume contraction inside the consolidation — it should tighten before the breakout, showing sellers/buyers drying up.

Entry, stop, and target

- Entry: on the break of the range boundary with volume expansion, or on the first pullback/retest of the broken level (higher win rate, requires patience).
- Stop: just beyond the opposite side of the consolidation, or beyond the retest low/high if using the pullback entry — this keeps risk tightly defined.
- Target: measured move (height of the consolidation projected from the breakout point) as a first target; trail the remainder using structure (prior swing lows/highs) if the move extends.

Common failure modes

- Chasing the breakout candle itself instead of waiting for volume confirmation or a retest — this is where most false breakouts trap traders.
- Trading breakouts from poorly defined, choppy ranges with fewer than 3 clean touches.
- Ignoring the higher timeframe — a breakout against the daily trend has a much lower success rate.

Worked example

A stock consolidates in a tight $18.40–$18.75 range for six sessions after an initial rally, with volume contracting each day. On day seven it breaks $18.75 on volume 4x average. Rather than chasing the breakout candle, you wait for the retest: price pulls back to $18.78, holds, and prints a small bullish candle. Entry $18.85, stop $18.60 (below the retest low), target $19.45 (measured move: $0.35 range height projected from breakout) — roughly 2.4:1 reward-to-risk.

Key takeaways

- Require volume expansion or a retest before entering — don't chase the first breakout candle.
- Define stop and target before entry using the consolidation's own structure.
- Only take breakouts aligned with the higher timeframe trend.

9. Mean-Reversion & Range Trading Strategy

The counterpart to breakout trading — profiting from price returning to fair value inside an established range.

The setup

- Confirm the market is in a genuine range, not a trend pausing before continuation (Chapter 7).
- Mark the range high and low as your two trade zones; the middle of the range is not a trade location.
- Prefer ranges with at least two clean prior reactions at each boundary — a single touch isn't enough evidence the level holds.

Entry, stop, and target

- Entry: at the range boundary, on a confirming candlestick signal (Chapter 4) or a momentum indicator showing overextension (e.g., RSI reaching oversold/overbought as price touches the boundary).
- Stop: just beyond the range boundary, sized so a false breakout doesn't take an oversized loss.
- Target: the opposite boundary or the range midpoint/POC for a partial exit — don't expect a breakout-sized move from a mean-reversion trade.

Common failure modes

- Fading a boundary that's actually breaking — always respect a stop; don't add to a losing mean-reversion trade hoping the range holds.
- Trading the middle of the range, where there's no defined edge in either direction.
- Using this strategy in a strongly trending market, where ranges are usually just pauses before continuation, not real reversal zones.

Worked example

A stock has held a $42.00–$44.50 range for eight sessions with clean rejections at both boundaries. Price rallies into $44.50, RSI hits 78, and a shooting-star candle prints. Entry $44.40 short, stop $44.75 (just beyond the boundary, 0.35 risk), target $43.20 (partial, near range POC) — about 1.4:1, appropriate for a mean-reversion trade where win rate should be well above 50% to compensate for the modest reward-to-risk.

Key takeaways

- Only trade the boundaries of a confirmed range, never the middle.
- Keep stops tight and just beyond the boundary — false breakouts are common and should be cheap.
- Don't apply mean-reversion tactics inside a strong trend.

10. Gap Trading & Pre-Market Prep

Gaps compress a lot of information (news, earnings, overnight order flow) into a single number. Trading them well starts before the bell.

Pre-market checklist

- Note the gap size relative to the stock's average true range — a small gap behaves differently than a gap that's 2–3x normal daily range.
- Check for a catalyst (earnings, guidance, news) — gaps with a clear catalyst behave more predictably than unexplained gaps.
- Mark pre-market high/low and the prior day's close, high, and low — these become your key intraday reference levels.
- Check relative volume (RVOL) pre-market — unusually high volume increases confidence the move has real participation behind it.

Two core gap strategies

Gap and go (continuation)

Strong catalyst, high pre-market volume, price holding above pre-market highs (gap up) after the open. Entry on the break of the opening range high with a stop below the opening range low; target using measured moves or trailing structure.

Gap fill (reversion)

Weaker or no catalyst, gap fails to hold pre-market highs/lows after the open, or the gap is unusually large relative to ATR with no news. Entry on confirmation price is failing (rejection at pre-market high/low), targeting a partial or full fill of the gap toward the prior close.

Worked example

Stock A gaps up 8% pre-market on an earnings beat, holds above its pre-market high through the open on 5x relative volume — a gap-and-go long. Stock B gaps up 6% on a vague press release, drifts back below its pre-market low in the first ten minutes on thin volume — a gap-fill short back toward the prior close. Same size gap, opposite trade, because catalyst quality and post-open behavior differed.

Key takeaways

- A gap's tradability depends on catalyst, size relative to ATR, and pre-market volume — not just that a gap exists.
- Decide between gap-and-go and gap-fill based on whether price holds or fails at pre-market extremes after the open, not on a prediction made before the bell.

- Mark prior close/high/low and pre-market high/low before the session starts — don't build these levels reactively.

11. VWAP Strategies for Intraday Entries

VWAP (Volume-Weighted Average Price) is one of the few indicators institutions actually reference for execution, which makes it genuinely useful rather than decorative.

What VWAP tells you

- It's the average price paid for the stock that session, weighted by volume — a real benchmark institutions use to judge whether their fills were good.
- Price above VWAP generally favors long bias intraday; price below generally favors short bias — treat it as a trend filter, not a standalone signal.
- VWAP resets each session, making it most useful on intraday timeframes rather than swing timeframes.

Two VWAP-based setups

VWAP reclaim/rejection

Price pulls back to VWAP after trending away from it, then either reclaims it with a confirming candle (continuation long) or gets rejected back the other way (continuation short in a downtrend). Stop goes just beyond VWAP on the wrong side; target is the prior swing high/low or a measured move.

VWAP mean reversion

Price becomes unusually extended from VWAP (measured using VWAP standard deviation bands). In range-bound conditions, an extreme stretch from VWAP with a reversal candle can be faded back toward VWAP. This is a range-market tactic — avoid fading VWAP extension during a strong trend day.

Worked example

Price has been trending above VWAP all morning. It pulls back and touches VWAP exactly, prints a bullish engulfing candle, and reclaims above it. Entry on the reclaim, stop just below VWAP, target the prior swing high — a textbook VWAP reclaim continuation long, taken only because the broader trend was already up.

Key takeaways

- Use VWAP as a directional filter (above = long bias, below = short bias) rather than a trade trigger by itself.
- The VWAP reclaim/rejection setup works with the trend; the mean-reversion setup only works in range-bound conditions.

- Combine VWAP with standard deviation bands to judge how extended price actually is before fading a move.

12. Building a Trading Playbook

A playbook turns the individual strategies in this book into a repeatable system you can execute without hesitation or improvisation.

What goes in a playbook entry

- Setup name and market conditions required (trend/range, timeframe, session time).
- Exact entry trigger — the specific candle, level break, or indicator confirmation required.
- Stop-loss rule and target rule, defined in advance, not decided in the moment.
- Invalidation conditions — what tells you the setup has failed before your stop is even hit, so you can exit early if needed.
- A few annotated chart examples of the setup working and a few of it failing, so you can recognize both in real time.

Limiting yourself to a small number of setups

- Master 2–4 setups deeply rather than dabbling in ten — depth of pattern recognition is what produces consistency.
- Choose setups that fit your personality: momentum breakouts suit traders comfortable with volatility; mean-reversion suits traders who prefer defined ranges and tighter stops.
- Every trade you take should map to a specific playbook entry — if it doesn't, it's not a strategy, it's a guess.

Worked example

A one-line playbook card: "Setup: Trend Pullback Long. Conditions: Daily uptrend, ADX > 25. Trigger: Bullish engulfing at rising 20 EMA on 15-min chart. Stop: Below engulfing low. Target: Prior swing high, trail after. Invalidation: Close below 20 EMA on 15-min close." Every trade taken under this setup should be checkable against this exact card — if it doesn't match, it doesn't get taken.

Key takeaways

- A playbook entry needs a specific trigger, stop rule, target rule, and invalidation condition — vague setups don't count.
- Fewer, well-mastered setups outperform a large, shallow collection.
- Every trade should trace back to a playbook entry; if it can't, don't take it.

13. Position Sizing & Risk-of-Ruin Math

Strategy determines whether you have an edge. Position sizing determines whether you survive long enough for that edge to show up.

The core risk rule

- Risk a fixed, small percentage of account equity per trade — commonly 0.5%–1% for intraday strategies, less for beginners or higher-volatility instruments.
- Position size = (Account risk in dollars) ÷ (Entry price − Stop price). This keeps every trade's dollar risk consistent regardless of the stock's volatility.
- Never size a position based on how confident you feel — confidence is not correlated with outcome on any single trade.

Why risk-of-ruin math matters

- At 1% risk per trade, it takes roughly 100 consecutive full losses to blow up an account — a near-impossible losing streak with any real edge.
- At 5% risk per trade, a losing streak of just 14–15 trades cuts the account roughly in half, and the math to recover gets exponentially harder (a 50% drawdown requires a 100% gain to break even).
- Oversized positions don't just risk more money — they distort decision-making, since fear of a large loss causes early exits on trades that would have worked.

Daily and weekly loss limits

- Set a daily max loss (e.g., 2–3% of account) that triggers a mandatory stop for the day — this caps the damage from a bad session or a broken mental state.
- Set a weekly max loss that triggers a step back to review the playbook and journal before resuming size.
- Loss limits should be non-negotiable rules, not suggestions you override when you feel like the next trade is a sure thing.

Worked example

A $30,000 account risking 1% per trade has $300 of risk available. The setup's entry is $52.00 with a stop at $51.40 — a $0.60 per-share risk. Position size = $300 ÷ $0.60 = 500 shares. If the same setup had a wider stop at $50.80 ($1.20

risk), the size would drop to 250 shares — the dollar risk stays fixed at $300 either way, only the share count changes.

Key takeaways

- Risk a fixed small percentage per trade and size positions off your stop distance, never off conviction.
- Small per-trade risk makes an edge survivable through losing streaks; large risk turns normal variance into ruin.
- Use hard daily and weekly loss limits to stop a bad session before it becomes a bad month.

14. Stop-Loss Placement & Trade Management

Where you place a stop is a strategy decision, not an afterthought — and what you do after entry matters as much as the entry itself.

Placing stops with structure, not arbitrary distance

- Place stops beyond a structural level (swing high/low, range boundary, consolidation edge) that would actually invalidate the trade thesis if hit.
- Avoid placing stops at obvious round numbers or exactly at the level everyone else is watching — give a small buffer for normal noise.
- If a technically correct stop makes the position size too small to be meaningful, the fix is a different setup or timeframe, not a tighter, arbitrary stop.

Managing the trade after entry

- Move a stop to breakeven only after price gives a real reason (e.g., a new structural level forms) — moving it on time elapsed alone is arbitrary.
- Scale out at predefined targets rather than deciding in real time whether to hold — this reduces the emotional load of watching an open position.
- Use a trailing stop based on structure (e.g., below each new higher low in an uptrend) once a trade is working, rather than a fixed trailing percentage that ignores what price is actually doing.
- A time stop — exiting if the trade hasn't moved in your favor within an expected window — prevents capital from sitting idle in a trade that's lost momentum.

Worked example

A long entered at $65.00 with an initial stop at $63.80 (below the setup's structural low) moves to $67.50 after printing a new higher low at $66.20. The stop trails up to $66.00 (just below that new higher low) — not to breakeven on a fixed percentage, and not because a certain amount of time passed, but because price itself created a new level worth defending.

Key takeaways

- Stops belong beyond real structure that invalidates the thesis, not at an arbitrary distance.
- If a proper stop makes the trade too small to matter, change the setup — don't shrink the stop.

- Manage winners with predefined rules (scale-outs, structural trailing stops, time stops), not real-time emotion.

15. Expectancy: The Only Math That Matters

Win rate alone tells you almost nothing about whether a strategy makes money. Expectancy is the number that actually matters.

The expectancy formula

Expectancy = (Win rate × Average win) − (Loss rate × Average loss). This tells you the average amount you can expect to make or lose per trade, in R-multiples (multiples of your risk) or dollars.

- A strategy with a 40% win rate and a 3:1 reward-to-risk ratio has positive expectancy: (0.40 × 3) − (0.60 × 1) = 0.6R per trade.
- A strategy with a 70% win rate but only a 0.5:1 reward-to-risk ratio has negative expectancy: (0.70 × 0.5) − (0.30 × 1) = 0.05R per trade — barely positive and easily wiped out by costs.
- High win-rate strategies (mean-reversion) and low win-rate strategies (breakout/trend) can both be profitable — what matters is whether the reward-to-risk ratio compensates for the win rate.

Costs that erode expectancy

- Commissions and fees, especially for high-frequency intraday strategies, can turn a marginally positive-expectancy system negative.
- Slippage — the difference between expected and actual fill price — is worse in low-liquidity stocks and during fast moves; factor it into backtests, not just live results.
- Overtrading (Chapter 1) dilutes expectancy by adding lower-quality trades that don't meet the strategy's actual criteria.

Worked example

System A: 42% win rate, average win $450, average loss $150. Expectancy = (0.42 × $450) − (0.58 × $150) = $189 − $87 = $102 per trade. System B: 68% win rate, average win $110, average loss $180. Expectancy = (0.68 × $110) − (0.32 × $180) = $74.80 − $57.60 = $17.20 per trade. System A has the lower win rate but is worth roughly 6x more per trade — win rate alone would have pointed you the wrong way.

Key takeaways

- Judge a strategy by expectancy (win rate combined with reward-to-risk), never by win rate alone.

- A lower win rate with a strong reward-to-risk ratio can outperform a high win rate with a poor one.
- Account for commissions and slippage when calculating real-world expectancy, not just the theoretical backtest number.

16. Trading Psychology & Discipline Systems

Knowing the right behavior and doing it under pressure are different skills. This chapter is about building systems that make discipline the path of least resistance.

Pre-market and pre-trade routines

- Run the same pre-market checklist every day (Chapter 10) so preparation doesn't depend on motivation or mood.
- Use a physical or digital checklist for entries — require every box checked before a trade is allowed, removing room for impulsive exceptions.
- Set a defined trading window (e.g., first two hours of the session) if that's when your strategies have the most edge, and stop trading outside it rather than searching for action.

In-the-moment discipline tools

- Use hard daily loss limits and trade caps (Chapter 13) as external circuit breakers — don't rely on willpower alone once you're already in a bad state.
- Say the trade's plan out loud or write it down before entering — externalizing forces you to notice if you're deviating from your playbook.
- If you notice yourself sizing up after a loss or a win "because it feels right," treat that feeling as a signal to step back, not act on it.

Handling drawdowns

- A drawdown within your backtested/expected range is normal variance, not evidence the strategy is broken — don't abandon a valid edge after a normal losing streak.
- Reduce size (not necessarily stop trading) during a drawdown to lower emotional pressure while you review what's happening.
- Review the journal (Chapter 17) to check whether losses came from valid setups that simply didn't work, or from rule violations — the fix is different in each case.

Worked example

A trader hits a five-trade losing streak that sits within their backtested expectation (their system has losing streaks of up to seven trades roughly once a quarter). Per their plan, they cut position size in half for the next week rather than stopping entirely or doubling down, then review the journal to confirm each loss was a valid setup that simply didn't work — not a rule violation. Size returns to normal once the review is clean.

Key takeaways

- Build routines and checklists so discipline doesn't depend on willpower in the moment.
- Use hard external limits (loss caps, trade caps) as circuit breakers rather than relying on self-control alone.
- Distinguish a normal statistical drawdown from a broken strategy before making changes.

17. Journaling, Backtesting & Continuous Improvement

Without data on your own trading, you're guessing at what to improve. This chapter covers what to track and how to use it.

What to log for every trade

- Setup name (from your playbook), entry/exit price, stop, target, and position size.
- A screenshot of the chart at entry, annotated with your reasoning.
- Whether the trade followed your playbook exactly, and if not, what deviated.
- The emotional state at entry (calm, anxious, revenge, bored) — this becomes a powerful pattern-finder over time.

Backtesting before risking capital

- Test a new setup on historical charts across at least 50–100 occurrences before trading it live, to get a real sense of its win rate and reward-to-risk.
- Forward test in a simulator or with minimum size for a defined period before scaling up — backtests are always optimistic relative to live conditions.
- Track results separately by setup, not just in aggregate — an aggregate P&L can hide one strategy that's working and one that's quietly losing.

The weekly/monthly review

- Calculate win rate, average win, average loss, and expectancy by setup, not just overall P&L.
- Identify your best-performing setup, time of day, and market condition — and consider concentrating more size there.
- Identify your worst-performing pattern (often a specific rule violation) and set a concrete rule to address it before the next review.

Worked example

A journal entry: "Setup: Gap-and-Go Long. Entry $21.40, Stop $20.90, Target $22.60. Followed playbook exactly. Emotional state: calm, well-rested. Result: +$0.90/share." Logged this way, a month of entries lets you filter: every gap-and-go trade taken while "anxious" or "rushed" might show a win rate 20 points lower than the same setup taken "calm" — a pattern only visible because the emotional state was recorded every time, not just on notable trades.

Key takeaways

- Log the setup, the chart, and your emotional state for every trade — not just the P&L.
- Backtest and forward-test any new setup before trading it with full size.
- Review performance by individual setup, not just in aggregate, to see what's actually working.

18. Building Your Personal Trading Plan

This closing chapter turns everything in the book into a single document you can follow every session — your trading plan.

The core sections every plan needs

- Markets and instruments traded, and the sessions/times you trade them.
- Your 2–4 core playbook setups, each with entry trigger, stop rule, target rule, and invalidation condition.
- Position sizing rule (fixed % risk per trade) and hard daily/weekly loss limits.
- Pre-market routine and daily checklist requirements before any trade is taken.
- Journaling and review cadence (daily log, weekly review, monthly deep review).

Treat the plan as a living document

- Update it based on journal data and backtesting, not based on a single good or bad day.
- Any change to the plan should happen outside market hours, during a scheduled review — never mid-session.
- Print or pin the plan somewhere visible during trading hours; the goal is zero ambiguity about what you're allowed to do in the moment.

Final checklist before you go live

- Have you backtested and forward-tested each setup in your plan?
- Do you know your exact position size formula and daily/weekly loss limits?
- Do you have a journaling system ready to use from trade one?
- Can you state your entry, stop, and target for a setup without looking at the chart first?
- If you can't answer yes to all four, spend more time in simulation before trading live capital.

Worked example

A one-paragraph plan excerpt: "I trade large-cap equities, 9:30–11:30 AM ET only. Setups: Trend Pullback Long, Range Fade, Gap-and-Go (see Playbook).

Risk: 0.75% of equity per trade, max 3 trades/day, daily loss limit 2.5%, weekly loss limit 5% (triggers a size-halving review). Journal every trade with screenshot and emotional state. Plan reviewed every Sunday using the prior week's journal — never mid-week." Short, specific, and checkable — that's the standard to hold your own plan to.

www.ingramcontent.com/pod-product-compliance
Lightning Source LLC
LaVergne TN
LVHW010739061126
851857LV00014B/1566